Design: Jill Coote
Recipe Photography: Peter Barry
Jacket and Illustration Artwork: Jane Winton,
courtesy of Bernard Thornton Artists, London
Editors: Jillian Stewart, Kate Cranshaw and Laura Potts

CLB 3513
This edition published in 1994 by
Whitecap Books Ltd., 1086 West 3rd Street,
North Vancouver, B.C., Canada V7P 3JS
© 1994 CLB Publishing,
Godalming, Surrey, England.
All rights reserved.
Printed and bound in Singapore
Published 1994
ISBN 1-55110-201-3

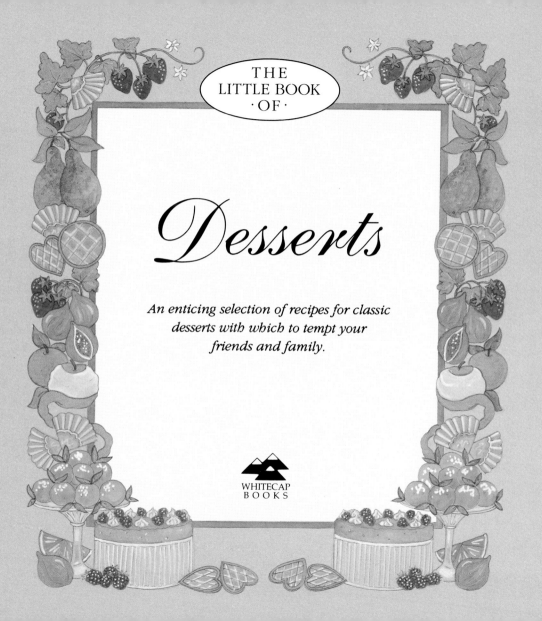

THE LITTLE BOOK ·OF·

Desserts

An enticing selection of recipes for classic desserts with which to tempt your friends and family.

WHITECAP
BOOKS

Introduction

For many people a meal is not complete unless it ends with something sweet, and they feel cheated if a dessert of some description is not offered. Though the current trend is indisputably towards cutting down on sweet foods, with fresh fruit, cheese, or low-calorie desserts replacing heavier puddings on a day-to-day basis, elaborate desserts still reign supreme on special occasions. A spectacular dessert gives the cook the opportunity to demonstrate his or her culinary skills and, as this will often be the part of the meal that people remember most vividly, will seal his or her reputation as a good cook.

The word "dessert," which comes from the French verb *desservir* meaning "to clear the table," is defined in the dictionary as "a usually sweet course served at the end of a meal." Desserts as we know them did not become commonplace until the eighteenth century when refined sugar, the basis of so many sweet dishes, became more widely available. Until this time, meals were usually completed with fresh and dried fruits, nuts, and cheese. The first, simple desserts were either pies and tarts, which used pastry or dough to encase fruit, or custards and syllabubs made by combining eggs with sugar and milk or cream. Desserts became more sophisticated as the demands of high society in the eighteenth and nineteenth century became more rigorous, and it was not uncommon for meals to end with a large variety of sweet dishes, including custards, pies, creams, cakes, pastries, meringues, gelatins, ice creams, and hot puddings.

Modern kitchen equipment, particularly electric beaters and food processors, have taken much of the hard work out of preparing desserts, and today's cook can produce some desserts in a fraction of the time that it would once have taken. More consistent oven temperatures and the ability to vary temperature at the touch of a button have also made it easier for the cook to produce the perfect result. This has meant that desserts that would once have been considered *haute cuisine* and would only have been attempted by an experienced chef can now be produced with relative ease at home.

This book features a selection of recipes for delicious desserts, including traditional American, Italian, and French specialties, with which to delight your friends and family. Ranging from the simple and relatively low in calories to the rich and utterly sinful, the recipes will provide inspiration for that all-important finale to your meal.

Parfait Au Cassis

SERVES 4

A rich and creamy dessert with a delicious fruity tang.

PREPARATION: 30 mins, plus freezing
COOKING: 30 mins

---

3 cups blueberries
2 tbsps blackcurrant liqueur
3 egg yolks
½ cup light brown sugar
1½ cups single cream
1½ cups whipped cream
Blueberries and mint leaves, to decorate

---

1. Purée the blueberries in a liquidizer or food processor, and push through a sieve with a wooden spoon to remove the skin and pips. Add the cassis to the purée and freeze until it becomes slushy, stirring occasionally to prevent large ice crystals from forming.

2. Whisk the egg yolks and sugar together until they become very thick and foaming. Heat

Step 2 Whisk the egg yolks and sugar together until they become thick and foaming.

Step 3 Cool the mixture quickly by standing the bowl in iced water.

the single cream in a small pan until almost, but not quite, boiling. Gradually add the cream to the egg mixture, stirring constantly.

3. Place the bowl over a pan of gently simmering water and cook, stirring constantly, until the mixture thickens. Cool quickly by standing the bowl in ice water, then fold in the whipped cream.

4. Freeze until the mixture is almost solid, then beat with an electric mixer or in a food processor until slushy. Break up the blueberry mixture with a fork or electric whisk and fold into the cream mixture to give a marbled effect. Divide the mixture between 6 freezer-proof dessert glasses and freeze until required.

5. Refrigerate 30 minutes before serving, and decorate with blueberries and mint leaves.

Apple Nut Tart

SERVES 6

The sweet, spicy flavor of cinnamon blends perfectly with the apples and nuts in this traditional dessert.

PREPARATION: 20 mins
COOKING: 40 mins

---

2 cups all-purpose flour
⅔ cup superfine sugar
½ cup butter, cut into pieces
1 egg
4 cups dessert apples, peeled, cored and sliced
½ cup hazelnuts, coarsely ground
1 tsp ground cinnamon
Juice of 1 lemon
3 tbsps apricot brandy (optional)
½ cup warmed apricot jam
2 tbsps chopped hazelnuts

---

1. Sieve together the flour and ½ cup of the sugar into a bowl. Rub in the butter until the mixture resembles fine breadcrumbs.

Step 4 Layer the apples and ground hazelnuts in the pastry case.

Step 5 Pour the melted jam over the layers of apples and hazelnuts.

2. Make a well in the center of the flour mixture and drop in the egg. Gradually incorporate the flour into the egg using a knife or, as the mixture becomes firmer, your fingers. Continue kneading the mixture together, until it forms a smooth dough.

3. Wrap the dough in plastic wrap and chill at least 30 minutes, then roll out and use to line an 8-inch greased pie pan.

4. Layer the apple slices and the ground hazelnuts in the pastry case. Sprinkle with the cinnamon, remaining sugar, lemon juice, and apricot brandy, if using.

5. Pour the warmed jam over the apple mixture, and sprinkle with the chopped hazelnuts. Bake in a preheated oven at 425°F, for 35-40 minutes or until the fruit is soft and the tart is golden-brown.

Mocha Ice Cream Pie

MAKES 1 PIE

Unbelievably simple, yet incredibly delicious and impressive, this is a perfect ending to a summer meal.

PREPARATION: 25 mins, plus freezing

12 Oreo cookies
6 tbsps melted butter or margarine
1 cup flaked coconut
2 squares plain chocolate, melted
2 quarts coffee-flavored ice cream

1. Crush the cookies with a rolling pin or in a food processor. Mix with melted butter or margarine.

2. Press into an 8½-inch springform pan. Chill thoroughly in the refrigerator.

3. Meanwhile, combine 4 tbsps of the coconut with the melted chocolate. When cooled but not solidified, add about 1 pint of the coffee ice cream, mixing well.

Step 2 Press the crust mixture into the base of a springform pan.

Step 5 Spread the coffee ice cream carefully over the chocolate-coconut layer and re-freeze.

4. Spread the mixture on top of the crust and freeze until firm.

5. Soften the remaining ice cream with an electric mixer or food processor, and spread over the chocolate-coconut layer. Re-freeze until firm.

6. Toast the remaining coconut under a moderate broiler, stirring frequently until pale golden-brown. Allow to cool completely.

7. Remove the pie from the freezer and leave in the refrigerator 30 minutes before serving. Push up the base of the pan and place the pie on a serving platter. Sprinkle with the toasted coconut. Cut into wedges to serve.

Zuppa Inglese

SERVES 6-8

The Italian name means English soup, but this is a rich, thick, creamy dessert.

PREPARATION: 25 mins plus chilling

2 tbsps cornstarch
2½ cups milk
2 eggs, lightly beaten
2 tbsps sugar
Grated rind of ½ lemon
Pinch nutmeg
4 cups ripe strawberries
16 finger cookies
Amaretto liqueur
⅔ cup whipping cream

1. Mix the cornstarch with some of the milk. Beat the eggs, sugar, lemon rind, and nutmeg together and add the remaining milk. Mix with the cornstarch mixture in a heavy-based pan and stir over a gentle heat until the mixture thickens and comes to the boil.

Step 1
Combine the custard ingredients and cook until the mixture thickens and coats the back of a spoon.

Step 3 Place a layer of finger cookies and strawberries in a serving dish and coat with a layer of custard. Repeat with remaining ingredients.

2. Allow to boil 1 minute or until the mixture coats the back of a spoon. Place a sheet of parchment paper directly on top of the custard and allow it to cool slightly.

3. Save 8 even-sized strawberries for decoration and hull the remaining ones. Place half of the finger cookies in the bottom of a glass bowl and sprinkle with some amaretto. Cut the strawberries in half and place a layer on top of the finger cookies. Pour a layer of custard on top and repeat with the remaining cookies and sliced strawberries. Top with another layer of custard and allow to cool completely.

4. Whip the cream and spread a thin layer over the top of the set custard. Pipe the remaining cream around the edge of the dish and decorate with the reserved strawberries. Serve chilled.

Raspberry Soufflé

SERVES 6

This light dessert is the perfect finale for a dinner party.

PREPARATION: 40 mins, plus chilling

4 cups raspberries
3 tbsps superfine sugar
1 tbsp unflavored gelatin
⅔ cup hot water
4 eggs, separated
1¼ cups heavy cream

1. Prepare a 6-inch soufflé dish by tightly tying a lightly oiled sheet of parchment paper carefully around the outside edge of the soufflé dish, allowing it to stand approximately 4 inches above the rim of the dish.

2. Reserve a few of the raspberries for decoration, and purée the remainder with the sugar in a liquidizer or food processor.

3. Rub the puréed raspberries through a nylon sieve to remove the seeds.

4. Dissolve the gelatin in the hot water, stirring gently until it is completely dissolved, and the liquid is clear.

5. Allow the gelatin to cool slightly and then beat it into the raspberry purée along with the egg yolks, mixing until all ingredients are well blended. Chill until partially set.

Step 1 Tie a sheet of parchment paper around the soufflé dish, to form a collar rising above the rim of the dish.

6. Whisk the egg whites until they form soft peaks.

7. Lightly whip half of the heavy cream into soft peaks.

8. Remove the partially-set raspberry mixture from the refrigerator, and carefully fold in the cream and the egg whites, using a metal tablespoon, blending lightly but thoroughly until the mixture is smooth.

9. Turn the mixture into the prepared dish – it should rise about 1 inch above the rim of the dish inside the paper collar. Allow to set in the refrigerator.

10. When completely set, carefully remove the collar, and decorate the soufflé with the remaining whipped cream and the reserved raspberries.

Coffee Pecan Pie

SERVES 6-8

This traditional American pie is ideal for serving after a celebration meal.

PREPARATION: 20 mins, plus chilling

1 cup crushed graham crackers
2 tbsps melted butter
1 cup pecan halves
1 cup marshmallows
1¼ cups strong black coffee
1 tbsp unflavored gelatin
3 tbsps hot water
1 egg white
⅔ cup light whipped soft cheese

1. Mix together the cracker crumbs and the melted butter. Press onto the base and halfway up the sides of a well-greased 7-inch springform pan and chill at least 1 hour.

2. Reserve 8 pecan halves for decoration, and chop the remainder finely.

3. In a large saucepan, dissolve the marshmallows in the coffee by heating gently

Step 2 Chop the remainder of the pecans.

Step 3 Put the marshmallows and the coffee into a large saucepan, and heat gently, stirring until the marsh-mallows have dissolved.

and stirring frequently.

4. Sprinkle the gelatin onto the hot water and stir until it is clear and has dissolved.

5. Carefully pour the gelatin into the marsh-mallow mixture, and stir well to ensure that it is evenly mixed in. Leave the marshmallow mixture to cool until it is almost set.

6. Whisk the egg white until it forms soft peaks, fold this into the whipped soft cheese, and then fold this into the marshmallow mixture, using a metal spoon to incorporate as much air as possible. Make sure all is evenly blended.

7. Stir in the chopped nuts and pour the mixture onto the chilled cracker base. Chill the pie at least 3 hours until completely set.

8. Remove the sides of the pan and slide the pie carefully onto a serving dish. Decorate with the reserved nut halves.

Chocolate Almond Stuffed Figs

SERVES 4

A positively luxurious dessert that is deceptively easy to prepare.

PREPARATION: 20 mins
COOKING: 25 mins

---

4 ripe figs
2 tbsps liquid honey
1 square semi-sweet baking chocolate
6 tbsps ground almonds

Cinnamon sauce
1¼ cups single cream
1 stick cinnamon
2 egg yolks
4 tbsps sugar
Ground cinnamon and blanched almond
  halves, to garnish

---

1. Make a cross-cut in each fig without cutting right down through the base. Carefully press the 4 sections of the fig out so that it looks like a flower.

2. Melt the honey and chocolate in a bowl over a pan of hot water.

3. Set aside to cool slightly and then mix in the ground almonds.

4. When the mixture has cooled completely, spoon an equal amount into the center of each fig.

Step 7
Combine cream and eggs and cook over gentle heat until mixture coats the back of a spoon.

5. Meanwhile, prepare the sauce; pour the cream into a deep saucepan and add the cinnamon stick. Bring to just under the boil, remove from the heat, and leave to infuse.

6. Beat the egg yolks and the sugar together until pale and thick, then gradually strain the infused cream over the mixture.

7. Return the mixture to the saucepan and stir over a gentle heat until it just coats the back of a spoon. Leave to cool until just warm.

8. To serve, pour a little of the cream onto each serving plate and tilt the plate slowly to coat the base. Place a filled fig on top of each and sprinkle around some of the ground cinnamon, topping each fig with a blanched almond.

Weinschaum

SERVES 4-6

This is a light and luscious dessert that can also be a sauce. Its name means "wine foam," which describes it perfectly.

PREPARATION: 15 mins, plus chilling

2¼ cups dry white wine
⅔ cup water
4 eggs
½ cup sugar
Orange zest or crystallized rose or violet petals, for decoration

1. Place the wine and water in the top of a double boiler over boiling water. Make sure the top half of the double boiler does not actually

Step 2 Check the base of the bowl or double boiler. If very hot, place in a bowl of ice water and continue whisking.

Step 2 When thick enough, lift beaters or whisk and draw a trail of mixture across the bowl. The trail should hold its shape.

touch the boiling water. Add the eggs and sugar and beat the ingredients vigorously with a wire whisk or an electric mixer.

2. When the custard thickens, it should hold a ribbon trail when the whisk or the beaters are lifted. Do not allow the custard to boil.

3. Spoon into serving dishes and decorate with strips of orange zest or crystallized flower petals. Serve hot or chill thoroughly before serving.

Frozen Lime and Blueberry Cream

SERVES 6

An impressive dessert that's perfect for entertaining.

PREPARATION: 40 mins, plus overnight freezing

Juice and zested rind of 4 limes
1 cup sugar
1 cup blueberries
3 egg whites
1¼ cups whipped cream

1. Measure the lime juice and make up to ⅓ cup with water if necessary.

2. Combine with the sugar in a heavy-based pan and bring to the boil slowly to dissolve the sugar.

3. When the mixture forms a clear sirup, boil rapidly to 248°F on a candy thermometer.

4. Meanwhile, combine the blueberries with about 4 tbsps water in a small saucepan. Bring

Step 5 Pour the sirup gradually onto the whisked egg whites, beating constantly.

Step 6 Fold the cream and the fruit purée into the egg whites, marbling the purée through the mixture.

to the boil and then simmer, covered, until very soft. Purée, then sieve to remove the seeds and skin, and set aside to cool.

5. Whisk the egg whites until soft but not dry and then pour on the hot sugar sirup in a steady stream, whisking constantly. Add the lime rind and allow the meringue to cool.

6. When cold, fold in the whipped cream. Add the purée and marble through the mixture with a spatula. Do not over-fold. Pour the mixture into a lightly-oiled mold or bowl and freeze until firm.

7. Leave in the refrigerator 30 minutes before serving or dip the mold in hot water for about 10 seconds. Place a plate over the bottom of the mold, invert and shake to unmold. Garnish with extra whipped cream and lime slices.

Tarte Tatin

SERVES 6-8

This classic French dessert is one of the tastiest ways of serving apples.

PREPARATION: 40 mins, plus chilling
COOKING: 20-25 mins

Pastry
2 cups all-purpose flour
1 stick butter, diced
1 egg yolk
2 tsps superfine sugar
½ tsp salt
2 tsps water

Filling
6 tbsps butter
6 tbsps superfine sugar
4 large tart apples, peeled, cored and quartered

---

1. To make the dough, sift the flour onto a work surface. Make a well in the center and add the remaining dough ingredients to the well, mixing them together with your fingertips.

2. Gradually draw in the flour, until the

Step 5 Neatly pack the apples into the skillet.

Step 6 Carefully lay the dough over the apples, tucking the edges down inside the pan.

mixture forms coarse crumbs. Add a little extra water if necessary.

3. Draw the mixture into a ball, then knead 1-2 minutes on a lightly-floured surface until smooth. Cover and chill 30 minutes.

4. Melt the butter in a 10-inch flameproof and ovenproof skillet, or tarte tatin pan.

5. Add the sugar and neatly pack in the apples. Cook 15-20 minutes, until the sugar caramelizes. Then allow to cool slightly.

6. Roll the pastry out to a circle slightly larger than the pan. Place it over the apples, tucking the edges down inside the pan.

7. Bake in an oven preheated to 425°F 20-25 minutes or until the pastry is crisp and golden.

8. Allow to cool in the pan 10 minutes, then turn out onto a serving platter and serve immediately with heavy cream.

Caramel Oranges

SERVES 4

This is one of the classic Italian desserts.

PREPARATION: 25 mins, plus chilling
COOKING: 25 mins

4 large oranges
1¾ cups sugar
1¾ cups water
2 tbsps brandy or orange liqueur

1. Use a vegetable peeler to remove the rind from two of the oranges. Take off any white parts and slice the rind into very thin julienne strips with a sharp knife.

2. Place the julienne strips in a small saucepan, cover with water and bring to the boil. Drain, then dry.

3. Cut the ends off all the oranges, then take the peel and white part off in very thin strips, using a sawing motion. Cut the oranges horizontally into slices about ¼-inch thick.

Step 1 Peel the oranges in thin strips with a vegetable peeler. Remove any white parts and cut into thin julienne strips.

Step 3 Use a serrated knife to take off orange peel in thin strips.

4. Stir the sugar and 1½ cups of the water in a heavy-based pan over medium heat until the sugar has dissolved. Add the drained orange peel strips to the pan.

5. Boil the syrup gently, uncovered, about 10 minutes or until the orange strips are glazed. Remove the strips from the pan and place on a lightly-oiled plate.

6. Return the pan to a high heat and boil, uncovered, until it turns a pale golden-brown. Remove from the heat immediately and quickly add the remaining water. Return to a gentle heat for a few minutes to dissolve the hardened caramel, then allow to cool completely. Stir in the brandy.

7. Arrange the orange slices in a serving dish, and pour the cooled syrup over them. Pile the glazed orange strips on top and refrigerate for several hours, or overnight, before serving.

Fresh Fruit in Tulip Cups

SERVES 4

Elegant presentation is what gives this simple fruit dessert its special, dinner-party touch.

PREPARATION: 10 mins, plus 1 hr standing
COOKING: 8-10 mins

Tulip cups
1 egg white
4 tbsps sugar
2 tbsps all-purpose flour
2 tbsps melted butter
2 tbsps ground almonds
1 tbsp flaked almonds

Fruit filling
1 mango
2 figs
10 strawberries
1 kiwi
10 cherries
Vanilla ice cream
1 tbsp flaked almonds

1. To make the tulip cups, mix the egg white with the sugar, then add the flour, melted butter, and the ground almonds, beating well to incorporate all the ingredients. Set aside to rest for 1 hour.

2. Peel the fruit as necessary and cut into attractive shapes.

3. Place 1 tbsp of the mixture on a nonstick

Step 5 While the cookies are still hot, mold them by pressing them into small bowls so they have crinkled edges.

baking tray, and spread it out well using the back of a spoon. Repeat three times. Sprinkle the flaked almonds over the mixture, dividing them equally between the four rounds.

4. Bake in an oven preheated to 400°F 8-10 minutes or until lightly brown.

5. When cooked, and while they are still hot, mold the cookies by pressing them into individual brioche pans or small bowls. Allow them to cool and harden in the molds.

6. When cool, remove the tulip cups from their molds and place on serving plates. Fill with the fruit, top with a little vanilla ice cream, and decorate with the remaining 1 tbsp flaked almonds.

Apricot Fool

SERVES 4

This dish makes a very quick and easy dessert.

PREPARATION: 10 mins, plus soaking
COOKING: 30 mins

---

1 cup dried apricots
1 ripe banana
1 cup thick-set plain yogurt
1 egg, separated
Chocolate curls or toasted, slivered almonds

---

1. Soak the apricots in water for at least 1 hour. Simmer in the water 20-30 minutes or until tender, then remove with a slotted spoon to a blender or food processor, and purée until smooth.

2. Mash the banana and add to the apricot purée.

3. Fold the yogurt into the fruit mixture along with the egg yolk.

4. Whisk the egg white until stiff, then gently fold into the fruit mixture. Spoon into individual dessert glasses and chill. Decorate with curls of chocolate or toasted almonds.

Poires au Vin Rouge

SERVES 6

A great way of using firm cooking pears to their best advantage.
They look beautiful served in a glass bowl.

PREPARATION: 25 mins
COOKING: 20 mins

2½ cups dry red wine
Juice of ½ lemon
1 strip lemon peel
1 cup sugar
1 small piece stick cinnamon
6 small ripe but firm pears, peeled, but with the
    stalks left on
1 tsp cornstarch (optional)
4 tbsps toasted flaked almonds (optional)
½ cup whipped cream (optional)

---

1. Bring the wine, lemon juice and peel, sugar,
and cinnamon to the boil in a deep saucepan
or flameproof casserole in which the pears fit
snugly. Stir until the sugar dissolves and then
allow to boil rapidly 1 minute.

Step 2 Peel the pears length-wise and remove the eye from the bottom.

Step 2 Place the pears in the simmering wine, upright or on their sides.

2. Peel the pears lengthwise and remove the
small eye from the bottom of each. Place upright
in the simmering wine. Allow to cook slowly 20
minutes, or until soft but not mushy. If the syrup
does not completely cover the pears, allow to
cook on their sides and turn and baste them
frequently. Cool the in the syrup until lukewarm
and then remove them. Remove the cinnamon
stick and the lemon peel and discard.

3. If the syrup is still very thin, remove pears,
boil to reduce slightly or mix 1 tbsp cornstarch
with a little cold water, add some of the warm
syrup and return the cornstarch to the rest of
the syrup. Bring to the boil, stirring constantly,
until thickened and clear. Spoon the syrup over
the pears and refrigerate or serve warm.
Decorate with toasted flaked almonds and
serve with lightly-whipped cream if wished.

Vanilla Cream Melba

SERVES 4

Pasta is wonderful in desserts as it soaks up flavors beautifully.

PREPARATION: 15 mins, plus chilling
COOKING: 10 mins

---

3 ounces small pasta shells
2 cups milk
3 tbsps brown sugar
Few drops vanilla extract
⅔ cup lightly whipped cream
1 large can peach halves
1 tsp cinnamon (optional)

Melba sauce
2 cups raspberries
2 tbsps confectioner's sugar

Step 4 Serve the pasta with peach halves.

1. Cook the pasta in the milk and sugar until tender. Stir regularly, being careful not to allow it to boil over.

2. Draw off the heat and stir in vanilla extract. Pour the pasta into a bowl and allow to cool. When cool, fold in the cream and leave to chill in the refrigerator.

3. Meanwhile, make the Melba sauce. Purée the raspberries in a blender or food processor, then push the purée through a fine nylon sieve. Mix in some confectioner's sugar to taste.

4. Serve the vanilla cream in shallow dishes. Set the peach halves on top and pour the Melba sauce over them. Dust with cinnamon if wished.

Step 2 Fold cream into cooled pasta mixture.

Lemon and Ginger Cheesecake

SERVES 6-8

This fresh, creamy-tasting cheesecake is full of wholesome ingredients.

PREPARATION: 30 mins, plus chilling

3 tbsps butter, melted
2 tbsps soft brown sugar
1 cup crushed wholewheat cookies
1 cup soft cheese
2 eggs, separated
Finely grated rind 1 lemon
2 tbsps soft brown sugar
⅔ cup plain yogurt
1 tbsp unflavored gelatin
3 tbsps hot water
Juice ½ lemon
3 pieces preserved stem ginger, rinsed in warm water, and chopped
4 tbsps thick plain yogurt

1. Mix the melted butter with the sugar and crushed cookies. Press the mixture evenly over the base of a greased 7-inch loose-bottomed

Step 1 Spread the cookie crumb mixture evenly over the base of the pie pan, drawing it slightly up the sides of the pan.

Step 4 Thoroughly mix in the dissolved gelatin, along with the lemon juice. Stir the mixture well, to ensure that the gelatin is evenly blended.

pie pan and chill for at least 1 hour.

2. Beat the soft cheese with the egg yolks, lemon rind, and sugar. Stir in the yogurt.

3. Dissolve the gelatin in the water, and add this to the cheese mixture, stirring thoroughly, to incorporate evenly.

4. Stir in the lemon juice, and put the cheese mixture to one side until it is on the point of setting.

5. Whisk the egg whites until they are stiff but not dry, and fold them lightly, but thoroughly, into the cheese mixture, together with the chopped ginger. Spoon into the prepared pie pan, smoothing the surface.

6. Chill the cheesecake 3-4 hours, until the filling has set completely. Swirl the natural yogurt over the top and decorate with matchstick strips of lemon zest, or lemon twists.

Summer Pudding

SERVES 6

This dessert must be prepared at least 24 hours before it is needed and is an excellent way of using up a glut of soft summer fruits.

PREPARATION: 30 mins, plus overnight chilling

6 cups mixed soft fruits (raspberries, blueberries, pitted cherries, strawberries)
8-10 thick slices day-old white bread, with crusts removed
½ cup superfine sugar (more or less can be used according to taste)

1. Prepare and wash fruits and place in a heavy-based saucepan together with the superfine sugar. Cook over a low heat until the sugar dissolves and the juices start to run.

2. Line the base and sides of a greased 2-quart heatproof bowl with some of the slices of bread, trimmed to fit the shape of the bowl tightly. Pack in the fruit and a little of the juice to stain the bread.

3. Cover with the remaining slices, pour on a little more juice, and retain the rest. Cover the basin with a saucer or plate which rests on the pudding itself.

4. Add a 1 pound weight or heavy can or jar, in order to compress the pudding. Leave to stand overnight in the refrigerator or a cool place.

5. To unmold, loosen the sides with a metal spatula and invert onto a serving platter. Use the remaining juice to stain any white patches of bread and serve with heavy or whipped cream.

Brown Bread Ice Cream

SERVES 4

This unusual ice cream is easy to make and is an ideal standby dessert to keep in the freezer.

PREPARATION: 40 mins, plus freezing

---

2 egg yolks
2 tbsps superfine sugar
2 cups heavy, or whipping cream
Few drops of vanilla extract
1 cup water
⅔ cup soft brown sugar
6 tbsps fresh brown breadcrumbs
1 tsp ground cinnamon

---

1. Put the egg yolks and the superfine sugar into a bowl, and whisk vigorously with an electric beater until thick, pale, and creamy.

2. Pour in the heavy cream and continue whisking until thick and creamy.

3. Beat in the vanilla extract, then pour the cream mixture into a shallow tray and freeze for 1 hour, or until beginning to set around the edges.

4. Break the ice cream away from the edges and whisk with the electric beater until the ice crystals have broken up. Return to the freezer for a further hour. Repeat this procedure two more times, then allow to freeze completely.

5. Put the water and brown sugar into a small saucepan and heat gently, stirring until the sugar has dissolved. Bring the mixture to the

Step 6 When cooled, the caramelized breadcrumbs should set completely hard.

boil, and boil rapidly until the sugar caramelizes.

6. Remove the caramel sugar from the heat and stir in the breadcrumbs and the cinnamon. Spread the mixture onto a baking tray lined with oiled parchment paper, and allow to set.

7. Break up the caramelized breadcrumbs by placing them in a plastic food bag and crushing with a rolling-pin.

8. Turn the frozen ice cream into a large bowl and break it up with a fork. Allow to soften slightly, then stir in the caramelized breadcrumbs, mixing thoroughly to blend evenly.

9. Return the ice cream to the freezer tray and freeze completely. Allow the mixture to soften 10 minutes before serving in scoops with crisp cookies.

Index

Frozen Lime and Blueberry Cream – an impressive finale to a special meal.